All These Restless Ghosts

Robert J. Levy

FUTURECYCLE PRESS

www.futurecycle.org

Library of Congress Control Number: 2014959379

Copyright © 2015 Robert J. Levy
All Rights Reserved

Published by FutureCycle Press
Lexington, Kentucky, USA

ISBN 978-1-938853-63-0

For Evan, Emma, Toby and my mother

Contents

Gorilla

Justly proud of his opposable thumb, this lustful simian
is only dimly aware of his ability to flex that digit,
of how it erects an industry of his yearnings, empowers
him to grasp the girl, the banana or even his own cock,

of how to clasp is to make personal pleasure feasible,
humanizing him in a way that crafts a reality of craving,
because, surely, it is the ability to make what is not ours
ours—to clutch to our bosoms the bright objects of our longing

—that draws us again to the lubricious paraphernalia
of the world. This monkey shines with the ambition to acquire
his bliss, and he does this despite the cages that confine him—
all the irksome workday humdrum of scratching, eating, shitting

and earning a living with his nearly human capering,
which keeps the flashbulbs firing. He clutches to his face a towel
(more a filthy rag saturated with feces and saliva,
a totem of desire and of the vast distance he must go

to slake his needs) and sits supreme in his pen, begrimed with mud,
eyeing admirers with an aching mix of hunger and hate
that can't help but make them feel belittled, shriven in his presence,
because he wants so much *to want,* and they, in turn,

would dearly love to want as much—with the pure bodily rage
that entails an entire lifetime's worth of fettered longing.
Were hope a thing with feathers, he would pluck them one by one,
making of each a trophy for his steaming, urgent pining,

which he snorts out in clouded breaths above his bearded muzzle,
daring anyone around him to hunger more than himself,
which is the cruel prison that surrounds him like a second hide
and hope's way of keeping him, and us, alive and desirous.

Earthward

Wouldn't we like to live as though a leaf
        were argument enough to set the world
ablaze, as though the murmurs from the trees
        were urgent memos from another world,
and isn't it the case that we cannot
        because we've tumbled, not from grace, but from
our naive selves, those good men and women
        we once were before our lives got in the way?

It's our dailiness, after all, that makes
        us what we are and melts our hearts,
that both inures us to the infinite
        and anchors us irrevocably in
a present mined with loss. Still, we rummage
        in the luminous dustheap for some sign
of first intent when our inheritance
        was starlight and applause. The tears we shed,

the laughs we laugh, are nowhere to be found
        amid such cosmic dross. Mired as we are
in a particulate sublime, we cling
        for life to the wreckage of a single
word, a living sound that signifies
        a world as damaged and transformative
as an incandescent fallen leaf,
        a place of first return. There is so much

out here that is impossible to hold,
        so much that falls away like leaves, and leaves
us desolate and shorn of hope; and, too,
        there is a glimmering, a surface
shot through with a sturdy, homely light,
        like candles guttering on windowsills
through an indifferent night. Day after day
        we accrue beauty and forfeiture,

night after night we sleep and let them slide
    back into the nameless blue in which we
all began. Wouldn't we like to live
    as though the least unanswered question
were a flame? And wouldn't we, flames ourselves,
    dry leaves upon a late-October tree,
gladly sputter and extinguish as we
    plunge earthward into immolating bliss?

If Only

If only my grandmother had wheels,
she'd be a trolley car, my father-in-law
intoned once, quoting his mother on how
people live in the conditional tense—
all the *shoulda, woulda, couldas* to which

we cling as to a precipice. He clung
a full year in the ICU, sepsis sucking
his heart dry. If only he'd had wheels he might
have motored to old Yankee Stadium,
revisiting the site of Lou Gehrig's

farewell speech (which he witnessed as a teen
playing hooky), recalling how one man
shed this glorious world with grace. If only
he'd had wings he might have plummeted
like a bluejay over the flowered fields

of his beloved Ghent, New York, eating aphids
that belabored his garden each summer,
knowing only the sky's ministrations,
all notions of mortality limited
to the absence of wind. Without wheels or wings

he was, instead, none of those things. All
the apparatus to which he was attached
left him grounded like a late summer fruit
too long on the vine, his bearish body
reduced to a parched sac, his humor slaked

by dementia, as though the man we knew
were drifting from our hands like jetsam.
The doctors, perhaps, *should* have done something,
and maybe they *would* have if they *could* have,
but he was no conundrum, just a thing

webbed in a net of drips and catheters,
unable to master his oncoming
finality. By his twelfth month he was
ready to depart. If only his too-full heart
had been able to bear three operations.

If only there had been redress. His flat,
now-alien eyes trembled one last time,
fixed on some far-off countryside to which
neither wheels nor wings could chevy him.
If only he could have seen us waving.

Cigarette

The best cigarette I ever had was the last,
if by *last* one means *final* (not *most recent*)
and by *best* one means *surpassing all others*
in excellence (i.e., *promoting longevity*);
however, if what is meant by *best* cigarette
is one savored repeatedly in memory
(despite adverse health effects), there would be

many contenders: such as one decades back
at the Village Vanguard while eavesdropping
on Sonny Rollins reinventing joy, shrewdly
dissecting the aural continuum,
as he soloed on "Don't Stop the Carnival,"
the smoke's sinuous fingers double-stopping
in the club's rich blue haze; and the one after

the poetry reading when a young woman
(who would become my wife) listened to me go on
about nothing for an hour, while I fell
into her jade eyes; and the one (which I may
be making up) with a college pal in Yellowstone,
drinking "near" beer, discussing Kierkegaard
because we were young, thought ourselves immortal

as we talked all night about the nature of "the good";
which brings to mind the whole question of *best*—
as in *best* book, *best* painting—where we argue
for absolute good (which we suspect is absurd),
pitting, say, *Magic Flute* vs. *Das Rheingold*
for finest opera, or "Tutti Frutti"
vs. "Day in the Life" for top rock song,

where we realize we would be impoverished
should we ever stoop to declaring "a winner";
so, perhaps, there never was a best cigarette,

perhaps there were many kinds, and such discussions
are, at last, a smokescreen for the inadequacy
of mere language to capture the lazy swirl of it,
the dance of it, and the collapsing worm of ash.

The Wrong Note

For Ornette Coleman

Listening this morning to Coleman unfurl
"Lonely Woman" on his white plastic sax
I recalled the old piano player
who said, "Whenever I hit a wrong note,
I just play it about three more times
and call it jazz." There is so much of life

that is like an accident made music,
sort of sonic penicillin, a cure
both serendipitous and insane.
Miscues may be that most fertile fraction
of ourselves, a kind of *ur*-correctness
both inelegant and sublime. Today

I listened to Coleman reel off inspired
furbelows of perfect errors until
I found myself swimming, drowning with him
in the self-same aural stew, and then thought
to write about it, about how it feels
to be dislocated by sound—taken

apart and put back together again
by honking piped in from the furthest rim
of sense. It's the rightness in the wrongness
that wrings an urgent inner ache, the thought
that's poignantly askew, that's teetering
on the dire fulcrum of what's possible,

that stays with us, blissed and unresolved,
the way Coleman's frenzied noodlings
flail a receptive ear with light so bright
it burns the rational like a laser,
which illuminates that lonely woman
sitting in a railroad flat, chain-smoking,

her seclusion chased by harsh, warm gin
and memory's cosseting self-pity,
the music rendering her exquisite
and compelling to the point where you want
to be the man who solves her solitude,
who makes her forget tense isolation,

and holds her bird-twig shoulders in your hands,
her tears soaking your shirt collar, the sounds
bathing you both in the calm lassitude
of aloneness, and all those wrong notes,
those beautiful, sanctifying wrong notes,
reassembling you as you start your day.

Skin

Plaques, dermatologists called them,
those desiccated flakes of me
which fluttered from my elbows, knees
and hands, as though each silver fleck
of detritus were a cenotaph;
but I was too busy shedding
myself into my own future
to venerate my past. *Poor skin,* I mourned,
investing those dry, little slivers
with a life apart. I could catalog

a list of regrets, like photographs,
with each shard of me that wafted
to the floor: This shaving's me
at 18, horny as hell, watching
a naked college girl (who'd one day
be my wife) do sit-ups in her dorm;
that shred chronicles my acrid divorce
from the same woman at 30; here
I am, this bit, at 35, embarking
on a ten-year lapse of confidence

in my facility to love. Dear skin,
all you poignant lost fractions:
If I could collect you together
and reassemble what I was,
I would engage you, my tissue golem,
in a dialogue about loss,
of how we misplace ourselves in time
with each success and every unrealized
goal. Then my second, hoary self—
lifelong companion of everything

I might have been—would no doubt scold
me through parched, onion-skin lips
for my self-defeating pity,
as though to say, *If I ever was you,*
I am not now; I have gone on
to lead a full life from your remnants,
and if you, my progenitor,
cannot construct a going-forwardness
from flesh and blood and bone,
you have yourself to blame. I still

lose smidgens of myself each day,
but don't we all? Isn't it, truly,
reassembling what we *were* that
makes us what we *are.* You need
a thick skin to lose yourself
in life (shedding the dermal slough
that surrounds you like a second coat)
to find yourself again, which is the work
of every day as we inscribe ourselves
on this thin and brittle human paper.

Sorry

Sorry, we say, thudding lumpishly into a commuter;
and sorry we aver, as well, jammed into elevators
ferrying us to cubicles where regret's our daily bread
(our *pain,* in French); and sorry, too, I suppose, is the sad mutt

who pees the rug and, in his doggy mind, is duly mindful
of absolute good and bad. There's much to be remorseful for
in this entropic surround. When a mere soupçon of regret
aggrieves us, we are bereft for that nanosecond of guilt,

and then we pass heedless into the hurly-burly of day's
dun exigencies as though sorry were a meaningless *mot*
tossed off like *Thanks* and *Later,* shards of non-language languishing
in humid air, unthought of, like empty cartoon thought balloons.

Sorry, however, begs to differ. It's the fleshy body
of our being in this world, enrobing us like a second skin
and, too, the skeleton that keeps us upright. How would we live
with no apologetics of remorse but as amoral

engines chuffing heedless through the dark? And there are times we mull,
I'm sorry I was ever born, and often we feel sorry
for the whole show: for ourselves, the decent selves we might have been.
I think sorry is sorrow's younger sibling, admonishment

for all the tiny wrongs we do; and it's forgiveness, as well,
as we reserve our true contrition for our larger miscues
and keep our petty penitence for the jabs, the bumps, the swirl
of lesser lapses in luck and fortitude. Sometimes lament

is all we have, as on those nights when the woman turns away
from you in bed in silent demurral, and you would explain
so much the sad words at your disposal cannot quite convey,
knowing you meant to say something, sorry you never said it.

Ad

The Rothko on my office wall is simply titled, "Violet, Green and Red."
Mornings, as I settle to work, it towers above me, a wordless ad

for vacations from the real world: three quadrilaterals stacked upon
each other, faintly ominous and remonstrative. I am working on

a financial ad, which fades away under my dozing fingertips
as I contemplate Rothko's vastnesses. He got it right, I think, the furtive lapse

of one color into another, all that hulking purple brutality
pressuring a swath of dark green and buoyed up by a vermillion sea

seeking ascendancy. I consider how the painting is a successful ad
for itself. It could sell one anything from god to the lack of a god:

the investment doesn't matter; it would be an irreproachable good.
The ad over which I labor stares at me, begging to be put to bed,

but Rothko's sheer gigantism makes me sleepy, or rather, ambitious
in a way I am not. I would rather lash the page with fantastic hues

than with tired, required verbiage about "new" and "improved." I would prefer,
in fact, to become violet, green and red, create an ad that did not refer

to anything in the world except the unending, insurmountable well
of colors that heave up from the mind in a relentless tidal swell

containing every human product there ever was or ever will be,
as though all of creation were being hawked simultaneously.

Debt

Debt is propped between us tonight, in bed
paging through our credit card statements,
tsking at our wild expenditures
on schoolbooks, groceries, galoshes
for the kids. My wife, half-perusing *Vogue,*
grows vague with inattention, gazing off
into the cobwebbed corners of the room
at Venetian jaunts and sprees to Cabo
we cannot afford. Debt gradually
woos her from her better self: In his scuffed
black bomber jacket he's that bad boy
women love to hate—switchblade lean,

a deck of Luckies rolled in his sleeve,
sporting negativity like mirror shades.
In bed he's a consummate acrobat,
manipulating her positions of defeat
to moments of ecstatic gloom.
It's no pedestrian *ménage a trois;*
I'm a mere voyeur to her bleak moods,
her diatribes on the *life-we-don't-have,*
things-we-don't-own and *ambitions-*
to-which-we-cannot-possibly-aspire.
I should, by all accounts, be livid—play
the jealous husband to the hilt, insist

he haul his Harley from our driveway
and vamoose. *Who's the man in black boots,*
Daddy? the kids inquire. I explain
that he's just Mommy's special friend
who moved in one day unannounced
to peruse the ledger of our losses.
Unmanned, I watch him ravish her
with inklings of the good life—front-row seats,
upscale bistros, diamond tennis bracelets

and fancy lingerie. How can I hope
to dislodge this interloper from our lives?
(Bribe him with the money I do not have?)

Of course, it isn't really riches
to which he aspires, but our company,
which he battens on, as lice coexist
with their hosts, plying them relentlessly
as both a food source and a home.
Debt is now my wife's true spouse, a husband
to her steadfast gloom. We're getting on
now that I refrain from insisting
life isn't so bad (reminding her we have
our health, our children and our jobs).
I've moved to the foyer, make my bed
upon the couch. Sometimes at night

I hear their heated couplings through the walls,
her distraught, abandoned moans of grief,
and think, *What if I were suddenly rich?*
Would he finally pack his bags and go?
Or is my wife's passion for him so firm,
his vise-like hold on her so absolute,
that he'd remain despite my newfound wealth,
help her prosper in her faithlessness?
Meanwhile, Debt has made himself at home,
the fridge a mess, clothes strewn everywhere,
wet towels moldering on the bathroom floor,
his hand outstretched, demanding next month's rent.

Spaghetti and Ketchup

No doubt a disgusting degustation,
it turned up with alarming frequency
on our dinette table when I was young--
butter-slicked, wormy strands bloodied with Heinz
alongside salmon croquettes or hot dogs--
and because it was what I *had* to eat
I grew to grudgingly respect, if not love,
those sweet, red, gummy masses of pasta,
which satisfied my raging hunger for carbs
even as they somehow repelled me,
reminding me of all we didn't have—

money, sophistication and good taste.
In later years I taught myself to cook:
cassoulet, choucroute garni and all
manner of pasta—*arrrabiata,*
ragu bolognese, puttanesca. Still
there were evenings when something in me craved
immersion in my own unwieldy past,
a need to feed at the trough of memory,
and, in secret, I would boil spaghetti,
assemble my gustatory nightmare,
and slurp up that nauseating potage,

warm boluses of sticky starch sliding
down my throat. Satiated and sickened
by this vile madeleine, this remembrance
of things pasta, I choked on earlier times—
the rank denials, bitter disparagements,
acid self-recriminations—a stew
so glutinous my gorge would rise
and I would race to rid myself of all
I had consumed and that consumed me
in great stomach-churning heaves so violent
I would lie there, sweat pouring down my face,

my history temporarily expunged.
Nowadays my fare is less explosive,
less food for thought than simple nutrition.
I eat to stay alive, and live to eat
each day that's thrown my way, as though the now
were the meat and potatoes of a life
lived within a present that was always tense
with doubt about its history. Unsure
of where to find my sustenance I scrounge
for scraps, devouring myself and all
that comes my way. My hunger grows and grows.

Delivery

Redolent of herring, onions and fear,
I schlepped the shopping cart
uphill, mortified, ashamed of my stained,
fish-fetid uniform, wary of *her*—
the housemaid who'd receive me and the part
I was expected to play once I gained

access to her apartment. (Abie,
    the unctuous counterman,
had winked, nudged me in the balls, before I'd gone,
explaining delivery boys at the deli
always got free blow jobs from this woman.
Like it was a perk. *You are in for one*

helluva tip, lucky guy.) How to demur
    and still remain a man
in my coworkers' eyes? I rang the bell
in trepidation. She opened the door
and stood before me. My imagination
surged steamily: She was sexy as hell.

 I slowly unloaded the groceries
    while she watched me, sloe-eyed,
a casual hand on her hip, lips parted
as though in mid-question. I met her eyes
fleetingly—wanting, not wanting. She said,
Yes. Sure, I wanted to say, then started

for the door, though not before she stopped me
    with an oddly chaste kiss.
You're young, you be good, she whispered and pressed
money in my hand. Back at the deli
I was greeted with a round of applause
and back slaps—unthinkable that I'd passed

up the opportunity for free sex
    from a sultry stranger,
though Abie, of course, suspecting my qualms,
smirked derisively. I went back to my tasks,
imagining her lips, felt relief, hunger,
two sweaty dollars clasped hard in my palm.

Under Covers

Nights channeling WQXR
under covers, I swam in blissful dark
accompanied by Vivaldi, Bartok
and the rest of the Basic Repertoire,

drifting languidly away from all those
who would drum me back to domestic
hubbub. Thus mantled, I'd listen to Bach,
his cello suites—argument and praise

that gracefully caressed the eternal
verities one note at a time. (Dad
didn't buy it, thought I was setting a bad
example for the family.) All that fall

I force-fed myself classical music,
a kind of transcendental helium
that might help me float into a stratum
far removed from the claustrophobic

tedium of my life in Queens. Mom
thought something was wrong with me. She was
right. Hiding from the cacophonous
din of household fights, the constant slam

of doors in discontent, I tunneled deep
into a world of wordless beauties
and worked to dismiss this life, take my ease
with Schubert and Ravel, songs I could keep

to myself while my family battered
its collective head against our fraught days.
Dad threatened to take my radio away:
He couldn't stand anything that mattered

to me, that divorced me from the shrill blast
of dysfunction. It infuriated him
that I did not participate in this grim
undermining of ourselves, but, at last,

he too relented, crawled under covers
every evening to watch TV game shows
he clearly despised, just his eyes and nose
visible, peeking furtively over

the quilt's edge. My sister and mother followed
suit: one with her dolls, mumbling in the night;
Mom with Christian Science texts, lamplight
illuminating secrets that glowed

with irrational righteousness. We
spent all our evenings under covers
by ourselves, estranged, inconstant lovers
caressing our own wounds. It was safe that way,

hunkered down in enlivening solitude,
the blankets demarcating our private
need. The silence in the house lingered late
into morning, but all night violins played.

A Capella

It means "in the manner of the chapel,"
and watching my son and your daughter sing
last night reminded me of that spare church
where we spoke our vows so many year ago
and of the ruined sacrament we made
of our love, and of all the sad duets

we composed together in those tense years
when neither faith nor forgiveness salvaged
us from our graceless selves. What fraught music
we made as, unaccompanied by doubt,
we sang our dirge of denial, argued
long into the night about the meaning

of life as though love were a seminar
on love where, in the end, all arguments
could not right our listing hearts. Listening
last night to our children singing, I was
caught up in that net of glorious sound,
in love again, briefly, with what we were

at our best, and when the music finished
and the applause died down, reminded
of the silence that ensued between us
in those waning years when our dark fumblings
and half-hearted lies worked to defeat us
even as we unhinged ourselves from all

we labored so hard to believe. Last night
was the coda of something sad and sweet,
an apartness that can never be breached,
and a strange affirmation that what was
cannot ever be again. *A capella:*
It means singing *sans* accompaniment,

and over decades we have done just that,
sotto voce, unheard by each other
as we navigated the remainder
of our lives with desperate hymns, through disparate days,
hearing our children sing our songs for us
as they became our instruments of praise.

Surfeit

Forget the fleet apparition
in a lambent spring-stung meadow
of velvet bucks or rapt visions
of yearlings outside your window

tonguing salt as delicately
as dowagers sip tea. This year
the ecosystem's gone awry:
Deer are scurrying everywhere

like cockroaches. Blithely heedless,
a couple troop across the lawn
to ravage the budding hostas and lilies.
Meanwhile, one small fawn

naively craps in the tool shed
after humping the bird feeder.
Gradually, the magic's fled
at first sightings, and the wonder

that accompanied them gives way
to a surfeit of miracle
and the sure knowledge that—today,
tomorrow, every day—they will

be there. Maybe if, one morning,
we woke to a new scarcity
of tracks, scat and the furtive scuffling
in the shrubs, all the mystery

would return and we would again
experience the pastoral
sublime. Bambi nibbling blossoms, sun
dappling her haunches, the rural

gone Disney. Or maybe we've found
that both *too many* and *too few*
are mere ploys for getting around
the fact that nothing will quite do

except the extraordinary.
So we devise language that's less
about deer than our desire to be
in constant unresolved surmise.

This morning I found some faint prints
near the dwarf plum. It's not deer,
I thought with growing excitement,
and began imagining bears

rummaging through the vegetables.
Or maybe hedgehogs. Or a fox.
Any redemptive animal
could suddenly become our luck

and do for us what deer once did—
surprise us with ourselves, be all
mysteries at once, make us glad.
Even an astonishing squirrel.

The Fool

After reading *King Lear*

My coming is peremptory as truth.
Like rude grass I ply my quiet way
into the sun. Those who walk on me
leave no mark but what is momentary.
I am what lives forever. I give way.

As a leaf settles, so too I take my place
on the world's ground floor, feigning direction
as a weather vane that takes its notions
from the wind or, lying, let the rains
wash me back to my crude element.

Lastly, I am a tree that fells itself.
There is no one to hear. Yet I make a sound
so loud that even those who seek to hang
this poor fool will be amazed. I am of the world
and when I die I drag the world along.

Teabags

Sad sack of pekoe steeped repeatedly
for thrift, it lolled on the trivet, cooling
in juices clear as tap water. Mother
used the same teabag for days. What she brewed
as the weekend neared was vestigial,
tannic memories flavored by Father's

departure, which kept her funereal
and meant we must always live as though poor.
When friends came by, I stashed it, embarrassed.
Sometimes I dreamed of a penury
so liberating I could hold my head
up high, knowing our poverty was real.

One night I crept into the kitchen, junked
the bag, and replaced it with a fresh one,
barely moistened, from the box. A whole week
I replayed that routine while Mother quaffed
real tea, not sepia-tinted water.
It ended when, scrounging in the cupboard,

I found a small tin can: Inside it were
The seven teabags I had thrown away.
Mother had fished them from the trash to use
when I was out, a way of whispering,
I'm poor. I'm poor. And I will live this dream.
As though life were a cup, and she the steam.

Sunday School

Mom yanked me out of Hebrew school so abruptly
I could almost hear, cartoon-like, the *yarmulke*
fly off my *keppele*. I *plotzed* at the prospect
of no more Pentateuch.

                   Little did I know she'd
signed me up for Christian Science Sunday school
where, in the humid church basement, I was harangued
a strict hour each week about the unreality
of pretty-much-everything. The world, our bodies,
each rheum and pain—all were forms of "error"
brought on by "incorrect thinking" and flawed belief
in this fallen mortal plane.

                 I wasn't ready,
however, for Mary Baker Eddy, her denial
of the corporeal. I had only recently discovered,
after all, marijuana and masturbation,
and from my teen vantage point the physical realm
was just fine. Between getting high and self-abuse
I didn't need *Science & Health* raining on my parade
with its dour assessment of our human lot
as a kind of mass illusion perpetrated
by our frail, unruly minds.

                 I liked my messy mind:
how it congenitally yoked disparate nonsense
into glimmers of a world inside this world
more real, more fertile and more physical—
and fraught, deliciously, with death's authority
to make each day into a desperate prayer.

                        Evil
and death were illusory, the teacher said,
a notion I couldn't buy even on sale,
and she sold it like snake oil.

                   Without corruption,
I insisted, without the lapse of seasons—

green going to gold, the rude beauty of mortality—
life wouldn't matter as much. In fact, our end,
I argued—the very fact that we weren't immortal—
haloed us with immanence more consequential
and profound.
                    Death, however, was a big no-no
in that basement, and I was reprimanded
repeatedly, viewed as a trouble-maker
trying to usurp her rule. When I got sick, as well,
it was my fault, a moral incapacity, the product
of a mind contaminated by "wrongthink,"
and the longer my cough or cold lasted, the longer
I ought to remain embarrassed by my frailty.

There came a time I'd had enough and refused
to go back to Sunday School. Mom—outraged, threatened—
administered punishment by keeping me
in the house on Sundays. I spent those afternoons
alone, smoking dope, self-pleasuring and writing,
digging trenches in the too-real world, and loving
their capacity to defend me from the shrapnel
of Mother's degradations.
                    She'd arrive from church
with stories of the transcendent, immortal realm
to which she'd briefly been admitted, wondering
if I'd learned my lesson.
                    I had: The dying universe
still burned crazily, stars always imploding somewhere
by pure chance, and I worshipped in my rickety church
where death and the common cold shed equal radiance.

Shrapnel

The fleck of shrapnel in his thumb began
emerging fifty years after the war,
jarring memories of the Korean
conflict tunneling up from the snug lair

where it had slumbered, painless, for decades—
livid remembrance bandaged by brave flesh.
We'd ask about Seoul, about the grenade
that had larded him with metal, the gash

it left on his hand, but it was thumbs down
on our queries. He was willing enough
to display mementoes, satisfy my son's
hormonal craving for facts about the rough

and tumble of war, his rifle and machete
rimed with rust (which my son chose to believe
was blood). Despite prodding, he was unready
to act as a trove of war stories, have

my children at his knee while he relived
the sad harrowing of a foreign land
for which he bore no animus. He believed
in truces, times to be buried. The wound

did not concur, as though the thick body
that had obscured battles deep inside him
for so many years deemed it its duty
to unburden itself of the mayhem

all that bloodletting had entailed. His thumb
ached for weeks as the sliver knifed upward,
and with it memories that had lain dumb
for a half-century. When it finally emerged

after bloody prodding with a tweezer,
a grim trophy, he held it up, a gesture
at once proud and imploring, as though he were
asking for forgiveness and unsure

if his personal war against his past
had at last ended. He gave it to my son
who clenched it hard in his tiny fist
as though it were a totem, a loaded gun.

The Weather Pig

...And whether pigs have wings...
—Lewis Carroll

Dad, what's a weather pig?
—My son, age 7

Our son abed, the time has come, my love,
to talk of many things—the weather pig,
for instance, and its queer predilection
for rain and sun and every in-between,
of how, in life's meteorologic
barnyard it's more than a childish miscue
but the muddy barometer by which
the lashing rains of marriage may be gauged.

Consider the pig as you loll near me,
after we've hogged each other for an hour
of rutted bliss within our nasty sty,
spent (like the money we never have,
lost to preschool and therapy), waiting
for that final life-changing miracle
which never comes. Mull over that porcine
sage of mutability, how he's mired

one instant in the muck, and then, the next,
takes wing, his gross, unlikely bulk aloft,
trailing brown streamers of manure and slop,
surfing the isobars to see what's next.
Like him, we're hip-deep in the lush ordure
of sex and loss, vaguely comfortable,
just waiting to burst upward into air,
unbound by all the pink and pillowed flesh

that weighs us down, mere sucklings in love's game.
No Wilburs reading spider webs for clues,
we're merely hams without a cure, and yet

the weather pig is real, at least as real
as countless headaches wives have conjured
in the marriage bed to fend off swinish
importuning. We feed it lavishly
and keep it fat, for unlike earthbound pork

it can sometimes rise to the occasion,
for, yes, the weather pig can still surprise,
flying so high it almost skirts the sun,
and the only clue it was ever there
is a pregnant void, a whiff of bacon
threading through our lives on buoyant mornings,
heralding the pig's survival, its ghost
calling us to another married day.

Selling the House

Tonight the haunting plaint of mourning doves
laves the landscape with its honeyed sorrow.
I am splayed on the lawn watching the sun
first flame vermillion, then bruise-purple. Bats

tumble, perform a spastic *danse macabre*
around the crumbling chimney. Through the firs
blue fireflies forge evanescent lightning
while cicadas whir in mechanistic bliss.

None of this will be again. This calm, fierce life.
This crepuscule. This peace. Dinner is done
(a last supper on the lawn of sweet corn,
mozzarella, tomatoes). The dishes

are stowed away; the children are on Facebook.
As though the house were in some ICU,
we monitor its flagging vital signs:
the stark arrhythmia of the boiler,

the aged plumbing's intestinal rattle,
the cry of old rafters like exhausted bones.
The FOR SALE sign on the lawn
is barely visible now, a catbird

perched atop it, mewing pitifully.
My family asleep, I meander
through the body of what was once a home
but is now a ship we are abandoning

to the elements. I feel the sea swell
of alien ownership engulf this place.
I hear them even now: kids gamboling
on the lawn, Frisbees crashing into windows,

the clatter of pans as dinnertime nears—
future ghosts of a domesticity

not our own. I walk outside where deer scat
pebbles the ground and wind riffles hostas

with the sound of paper being crumpled,
as though everything we'd ever written
about this home upon our hearts were trash,
revision upon revision destined

for the dust bin. The sere late-autumn grass
sighs beneath my feet as I trudge back in
to where the house lies somnolent, oblique,
a 1790 antique waiting

for the next batch of interlopers to claim
its post-and-beam construction as its own
demesne. Half asleep upon the sofa,
I listen to the sound of our absence,

as though the walls already said farewell,
as though its soon-to-be-untenanted space
had emptied itself of all human thought
and resigned itself to merely being a cave

for bric-a-brac and revenants. Evening
collapses around me like a velvet glove.
Outside lascivious branches tongue the house
as though it were a sweetmeat. Distantly

feral dogs *halloo* their morbid night song,
serenading us wakeful where barn owls
watch us like some monstrous mouse.
Tonight we are prey to a homelessness

beyond mere walls, and sleep comes not at all
to those of us who would still build a house
of memories. We're drifting out to sea.
The mourning doves are in ascendance.

The Cancer Chef

The note informing me I had oral cancer
came in a glassine-windowed envelope
I nearly discarded as junk mail. Over
and again I read those lines leaching hope

from my days: *Squamous cell carcinoma,*
they brayed. ("Squamous" was such an ugly word,
mashing *squalid* and *infamous,* a
squishy death sentence.) Never before had

I hungered so much to endure. Over
the ensuing months radiation, chemo
and a pap-filled PEG tube in my gut were
my sustenance. Food was out. Oxycodone

and fentanyl rendered me ghostly
as I luffed on a white euphoric wave.
With my neck stitches, the children called me
"Frankenstein." My wife cowered as I hove

to the receding shoreline of my life.
For months I lost weight, read all of Proust,
had no remembrance of things past. My wife
marched the kids to school, laundered, stressed.

I fought back, trying to override the pills.
I remember vaguely rising from my bed
to cook a meal of salmon and lentils,
my family gawking at me like I was mad.

Next I baked pineapple upside-down cake.
What's with Dad? the children whispered to Mom.
For days I shambled about, a phantom cook.
Though still unable to swallow a crumb

I was consumed by food as my throat healed.
I churned out *ragu Bolognese,* meat loaf,
shrimp a l'Indienne, a flurry of meals
out of some queer desperation to stave off…

what? I still couldn't eat. Gastronomy
seemed merely perverse. Yet, food was bliss,
like a luxurious new discovery.
I expended my semi-comatose days

stove-bound, grilling lamb chops and boiling rice,
a way of re-engaging with a life
which I was sure I'd left. It was a race,
almost, though not against time. It was as if

the very *feel* of food—an egg's rondure,
a raw steak's spongy give, the gentle fur
of the kiwi—afforded me a rapture
of calm. As I slowly grew healthier

my need to cook receded to a dim
memory of mania. The children
grew less afraid. I could hear my wife hum
as she went about housework. One morning

she insisted on making breakfast
for me. I sat down on still-wobbly legs—
my hands itching to prepare a repast—
and gratefully received my toast and eggs.

Aftermath

In memory of P.L.

Compassionless winter scoured the landscape
of all things lush or intimating life
so our hoped-for Spring retreat became a dirge
in mottled brown: scraggly, ruined branches

strewn across the lawn like dead men's bones;
trees with dowager's humps; the deck destroyed
where icicles had plummeted like missiles,
smashing the bird feeder and chaise longue.

The fallow house breathed a funereal hush,
so we slept in, unable to rouse ourselves
for leaden afternoons promising nothing
but combing the lawn for wreckage. We tried

to make a game of it: Who could collect
the most twigs? Stooped low like Millet's gleaners
we were unpaintably sad, gathering
gnarled kindling for fires we could not ignite

within us. *Some vacation,* my wife complained.
Still, there was unlikely liberation
in putting the debris to rest, a strange calm
as after funerals (we'd had our share)

when turning away is also turning towards
what remains—the turbid, mournful keening
of a gray, unthinking wind though tree limbs;
the misplaced explosion of a robin

on the lawn—all of it a reminder
that both the death of seasons and of friends
is as one: reluctant celebration
of a vast and fractured continuance

we must embrace if we are to live with
the brute heaviness of going forward
into each day's night with a soft shining.
So we labored all that bleak March day,

speaking little, dragging ice-scarred tree trunks
to the shed for fitful sawing into logs.
When evening came at last (Thank god for night!)
we went about our disparate duties,

feeding our bodies, putting out the trash,
playing Bach, Mozart until we sickened
from the beauty of it. How could such sounds
fill this arched and timbered space with anything

but death, and how could we not acknowledge
that in this music was a ghostly noise
of tramping feet continuing their rounds
and making sure the house was shut up tight?

That night we made a fire of our achievements
—twigs and branches collected through the day—
and sat silently near the hearth, huddled
in a queer radiance that shed no warmth.

Vanishing House

Shucking sweet corn on the lawn, washed in evening's bruise-blue light,
moist silk clinging to our fingers like a last handhold on summer,
assembling dinner as we'd done a hundred times before, we noticed
the house was beginning to vanish, its post and beams barely visible
through panes of panoramic glass as it slowly faded from sight.

We went on slicing zucchini, eggplant and heirloom tomatoes
for ratatouille, pretending nothing was amiss, but we all
saw the timbers going ghostly in the twilight, not darkening
but actually losing substance, ephemeral in the rapt dusk.
We had acknowledged for some while the house was leaving us:

items had disappeared; mice and bats had been roosting in the rafters;
carpenter ants reclaimed the wood; and the rotted retaining wall
had collapsed into the rude patch of wild rhubarb edging the road.
The money wasn't there to save it from itself, from entropy's
tireless deconstructions. We watched its slow going as one observes

a boat evanescing over the horizon line. Still, the kitchen
was just solid enough for us to finalize our evening meal,
so we collected our simple repast and settled on an old bedspread
laid out on the grass. Together we shared our last supper facing
what remained of the house, its frame strangely beautiful, winking out

until, the meal finished, we were left at last in an empty field.
We felt the deer gather around, heard the mourning doves trill our loss,
and knew we could give in to it so easily, this vanishing
of all those soft summers we'd spent watching each other grow older,
the spare winters we'd huddled down beneath comforters listening to

the house settle into itself as the wind raged outside its walls
and the outer darkness closed in like a thick velvet glove,
so we began picking up twigs from the lawn, rough logs and smooth stones,
fashioning a cairn of sorts from what was left of our small lives,
piling them up like a rude altar as we began to build again.

Bypassed

Juggled with such dexterity, this beating heart
could be a mock-up used to teach biology,
and the team of doctors—moments before
a pack of fresh-faced med-school grads
one could as easily imagine skiing
as trephining—is now solemn,
druidical and clean as they prepare
for the rite of final closure.

As though TV had anesthetized me
to the livid, meaty fact of a heart,
I could not quite swallow what I saw,
like my old-world grandfather at 90
watching the first man walking on the moon:
Vat iz dis television, he said, outraged,
to show zuch lies? I vill go now
to de kitchen for zum milk and cookies...

The kitchen is white, white like the heaven
of every child's imagining,
unsurgical with the smell of new-baked bread.
I'd also turn to milk and cookies,
to reruns of sitcoms gone so stale from overviewing
I can laugh before the joke is told,
every line fresh with redemptive certainty
right from the opening, "Honey, I'm home...."

They prepare to reinsert the heart.
Between outer spaces and this inner world
of slick, unending surfaces
my grandfather and I would have stood amazed.
By the time the tubes are cut away
and the chatty commentators declare
the operation a complete success,
I have already drained the glass.

Theft

The Christmas ornament I stole
on a dare when I was thirteen
still afflicts me, burning a hole
in my pocket as though it had been

secreted there yesterday—cheap
tinseled doodad, quite meaningless
and garish, a macho keep-
sake that permitted me to pass

muster on the street. I felt ill
at my weakness, how I'd succumbed
to peer pressure, a kind of fall,
however small, from grace. Not damned,

exactly, but lessened in my eyes,
I hid the globed decoration
under my bed for seven days,
as long as it took for creation,

and then, my little world in hand,
I trudged through snow back to the store
from which I'd pilfered it. I planned
to put it back. Under the glare

of the floor manager I palmed
it from my pocket to the shelf
and felt unburdened, like a balm
had been applied to my wounded self

until a thick hand grasped my neck.
The manager hauled me roughly
to his office. Completely sick
I sputtered incoherently

about my attempted redress
of my wrong, but who would believe
my story? I wouldn't. At last,
after an hour, he let me leave

with stern remonstrance and a threat
to tell my parents if ever
I set foot in the store again. Late
that night I slumped in my room, never

to steal again (except, of course
for the pointless penknife I'd taken
as I'd sidled down the store aisles
on my way out, a kind of token

to remind me what I'd absconded
from myself, my sense of wholeness
permanently injured). I wondered
as I sat there in the darkness,

gouging divots from my bedpost
with my blade, how each piece felt like
guilt in my hands, parts of a past,
things that I could take and take and take

and never return, each chunk of wood
a gout of flesh, a kind of theft
of everything in me that was good
until no part of me was left.

Cleaning House

Just when do mere clothes devolve to laundry,
or dust motes mutate into "bunnies,"
and when do we—scouring and furbishing
our way to domestic pristinity,

become mere janitors to our own lives,
as though we never quite existed *now*
but in some forever immaculate
future? *Why doesn't neatness prevail?*

Yesterday I had hoped to clean house,
stave off again the creeping anarchy
of dirt over my days. Today I see
I've failed. Washing mounts ineluctably,

the teeming detritus of daily life
overflowing the prim wicker hamper,
burgeoning through the windows like sci-fi
protoplasm gone berserk, spilling forth

untidily down Main Street, trumpeting
my failure to stem entropy's cold tide
and tendency to ever-greater mess.
Clean is a dream, as unlikely as love

and just as hard to maintain. I mop
my brow as I scrub the linoleum,
envisioning the splatter and footprints
to come—from me, my wife, my children

forever begrimed—generations of stain
as encrusted as the genetic code
of the race. *Come clean,* they say in *films noir,*
bullying some felon to admission of guilt,

but the truth is we cannot lave ourselves
free of this world. We are all culpable
and exonerated, besmirched and rinsed
by each rueful attempt to make it new

or whole or virginal once more. Today,
in the insulting dazzle of morning,
it's all dingy, flecked with imperfections,
though not wholly uncomfortable, like clothes

worn so thin they've become a second skin,
like the grand living room window I've cleaned
and cleaned only to discover, at last,
a gray, obscenely necessary smudge.

Insomnia

Despite "sleep experts'" advice, I prefer
toughing it out, tangling with insomnia
as though it were some inky cephalopod,
wrestling its cold black body to the floor,
even though all that tussle leaves me drenched,
palpitant, ready for more. Wakefulness

is like that: a raw angel in the head
that caroms fitfully, craving coffee
at 3 a.m. when mere oblivion
is all you really seek. Sleeplessness
is that bedfellow pulling the covers
off your head, demanding conversation

and applause. It is best to ignore it,
head to the kitchen for a glass of milk,
or pick up a copy of *Clarissa*
until your eyes begin to droop. That's when
the soft susurrus of the bedroom calls,
and when, too, on the short portage between

rooms, carrying the boat of exhaustion,
that feckless angel brings you espresso
in the form of fear that you will never
sleep again. At some point, of course, we all
fall asleep, otherwise we'd die. But sleep
is a kind of dying, too, which is why,

perhaps, we fight it tooth and nail , averse
to the small, subversive deaths of dreamtime.
The trick of insomnia is despair:
it entraps you there, your head a tom-tom,
and your hands awrithe, and the taunt of sleep
a sigh heard dimly from another room.

Little Entropic Prayer

To the small god of mere continuance
I offer my hands at work, my children
at play, my wife's impassioned reluctance
to admit our daily limitations.

Sometimes I do not know how we go on,
hearts athrum in our tiny chests, ticking
off entropy's lapse, its slow religion
of little pyrrhic victories making

us muddle on through dire uncertainty
and pain. To the deity of forward
momentum I bring my small flesh ampoule
of blood, I bring my heart, its flaccid drum

of muscle always one soft beat away
from cadencing. In these lapsing days
mingling solace and discontent, I can
see, albeit dimly, the leaf depend

from the tree, just a temporary guest
a gust of wind could disinvite. To the
power that compels us into our night
I offer the meals I make my children,

the food of the land, the food of my thoughts,
neither of which can rewind the watch spring
of our days as we settle together
in peace and look up wanly at the stars.

Evolution

In Yellowstone, after Old Faithful, we unearthed
the New Faithful: scrubbed teen evangelicals
who let us share their campsite one rainy night

when the park was full. My friend and I
had been drinking Coors all day, and hailed from New York,
which made us prime candidates for redemption.

At night they sang folk songs around the campfire,
and we joined ironically in "Kumbaya"
while they spoke interminably of Jesus

as though he were part of their caravan.
Blitzed on beer, we wondered if we had a chance
with the cuter girls, could find our way into

their Christian pants because we were "exotic"
deflowering Jewish demons from the Northeast.
High on superiority to these rubes

from Montana, we were college boys brimming
with arrogance, cross-country pilgrimage
and the notion of "discovering ourselves"

and America. What we discovered,
instead, was another America,
one where Christian teens who had been strung out

on drugs and alcohol debated sin
and salvation while toasting marshmallows.
Late that night one acolyte approached me

to discuss, of all things, Darwin's folly
in believing we had come from monkeys.
With his brow ridge and sloped shoulders,

he was an oddly simian argument
for evolution even as he preached
to us the truth of creationism.

Still, they were a community of sorts,
and we slept on their fringe in our tube tents
listening to the rain and the geyser's

rhythmic hosanna gush, debating
the rightness and wrongness of everything
we had held dear and how, here in the woods,

we were at their mercy for food and drink
and companionship as we fell asleep
beneath the stars' obliterating hush.

Playground

Dead rat clamped in its jaws, the fat squirrel
scrabbles past see-saws, clambers up an oak,
and deposits its prize in a hollow bole,

almost insouciantly, as though storing
an acorn. It chitters out victory
from its high aerie, as though declaiming

in squirrel: *We all eat our own.* Below,
oblivious, toddlers gambol on swing sets
and sliding ponds under the watchful gaze

of nannies who manage feeding time with
Zip-Loc bags aswim with cheddar goldfish.
The squirrel busily revisits its cache

in a box hedge abutting the playground:
Amid the horrified, unwilling stares
of mothers who collectively refuse

to believe that this, too, is nature,
it retrieves a second rat, stockpiling
it with casual, businesslike mien.

Gradually the playground grows silent.
The gazes of children, nannies, parents
follow the squirrel as it diligently

pries another dead rat from a drainpipe
near the sandbox. Newly nervous, mothers
bustle, collect their charges near their skirts,

as though worried that, empowered, squirrels
might start making off with their progeny,
potential carrion to help stave off

even the severest winter. Clutching
strollers like battering rams, the parents
retreat from the playground-turned-killing-field,

avert their children's faces from the carnage.
*Mommy, how come mouses is eating
other mouses?* Might as well ask why

the park is empty now, save for a lone squirrel,
its taut body a rude exclamation point
silhouetted against the monkey bars.

Gatorland, Orlando, Florida

So garish, so outlandishly redneck,
so un-Disney: We simply had to go.
Even the entrance was implausible—
mammoth, gaping gator jaws ingested
visitors like prey. Devoured, surrounded
by black saurians, we felt transported
to the Mesozoic. Even the schlock
that peppered us (signs gave out monikers
like "Ol' Dog Eater," "Monstro," "Mega Jaws")
seemed a desperate, inadequate language

that failed to tame the leathern boats idling,
unperturbed in artificial brownish muck,
quite oblivious to gaping tourists
who aimed their Canons like futile weapons.
I admired these monolithic monsters,
gutting out evolution with tooth and tail
(plaques said they hadn't changed substantially
in 200 million years) and pitied
them, as well—those hunkering green boulders
mired in their synthetic bog, leftovers

from an eon when they ruled a world. Hundreds
were crammed into a crazy quilt of pens
in a steamy, mosquito-infested daze.
Untroubled, small birds rode their heads, ferried
languidly to one shore and back. It was
surreal and oddly sad—like a lost world reclaimed
only to be lost again—especially
the albino gator, a rarity,
1,000 pounds in a glassed mini-booth
more sump than swamp, which we watched do nothing

regally for fifteen minutes until
my children asked if he were dead. Speaking
of dead, the highlight of the day: watching
workmen wade into the middle of the swamp
to remove one that had recently expired.
It took a half-hour for them to line-drag
its putrid, sopping carcass to the shore.
It lay there noble and immense, just meat.
And speaking of meat, we passed the café
which proudly featured deep-fried gator bites

and freeze-dried bags of Cajun-flavored gator jerky,
as though Gatorland were both zoo and farm
where nothing went to waste, as though to eat
the primal past were to take in eons
of ferocity, so we could pride ourselves
in a kind of pathetic victory
over the feral sublime. "That was cool,"
my kids said at day's end. We headed through
those selfsame concrete jaws, which spat us back
on the hot street as though we were rancid flesh.

Goal

My son asked me to write a poem about him
playing soccer—not just any poem
but one about scoring the winning goal
in the final seconds of the second half

to the raucous sideline adulation
of parents and teammates. I would have
obliged, but found myself thinking about
a very different sort of poem—

this one, in fact, about him *asking me*
to write the poem. It's a betrayal
of course, the scenario ironic
as he never intended it to be,

but it's fidelity of sorts, as well,
a prayer to the interconnectedness
stitched into every passing thought
if not to my son's self-eulogizing intent.

My goal that week becomes teasing out
the simple human desire to become
a trophy of one's self, how we will thieve
from anyone we can to satisfy

our pervasive need for rumor
and applause. Days later my son
asks me, *How's the poem coming along?*
How do I explain it's doing fine,

even though it's no longer about him,
but a rueful meditation
on how you take what chances life
sends your way and run with them, madly,

making something new and strange and lovely
in their stead. How do I explain to him
that my poem is nearly complete
but his goal is forever unrealized?

Gray Interior

After a photograph by Philip Traeger

Imagine an abandoned villa, white
in voluptuous Veneto sun. Inside
all is bare. No furnishings intimate
a human presence. Each lime-washed façade

echoes the adamantine thoughts of stone
conversing along walls in swaths of light
that limn a stark reality: bone-
white, lead-gray, surfaces barren as slate,

a pale panoply of colorlessness
that only the mind of Palladio
could conceive as a rich wilderness
of habitability. Imagine, too,

the merchant traversing its spare spaces,
trafficking in exotica—damask
and saffron from the Far East, spices
scenting the vaulted archways with thick musk—

and how he, his plump wife, all his labors
shrink in comparison with the steel glint
of calm luminosity the corridors
breathe forth. Imagine the late-evening slant

of warm sun bathing the interior,
ebbing rays illuminating blank space,
slowly revealing the ulterior
purpose of this place—a way to erase

the mere human in favor of wan light
and the perfect geometry of stone
so that the inner softness of marble might
express itself. Imagine the merchant, done

with his day's work, abed with his sweet wife,
dreaming the dream of ownership, his abode
surrounding him like a second life,
indifferent as the rock is to the spade.

A Hole in the Wall

Furious, he kicked a hole in the wall
one night; we watched him extricate his foot
from the plaster crater. Thus Father could will
us to silence with a gesture. Of late

he'd been on a rampage. We said nothing
about the hole, which remained for weeks
a kind of abstract wall art representing
our dysfunctional lot. No one would speak

about it, but when everyone was gone
I'd place my ear to the wall to listen.
What was I hoping to hear? The wan sound
of the sea's susurrus as it intones

loss in the whorl of a shell? The murmur
of another world? Instead, what I heard
was this world fed back to me in a slur
of muffled talk. Lackluster moans in bed,

sharp cries of *Bitch!*, accompanied by blows,
and once, distinctly, *Not meat loaf again!*
Behind it all there was another noise,
like a hornet buzzing, a stifled whine

of animal violence. It could have been
just the commingled sounds of the building,
the boiler and the elevator in
diurnal tasks. But I couldn't help thinking

it was my father's fury, trapped inside
unforgiving gypsum board. It had gone
among two-by-fours and penny nails, hid
roughly among roaches and mice, alone

with itself and half insane with no one
to vent its wrath upon. Meanwhile, Father,
as usual after a conniption
fit, retreated to a passivity more

taut than conciliatory. At last
the superintendent patched up the gap,
trapping my dad's residual rage. We passed
solemn weeks waiting for the next mishap

to send him ballistic. I would rather
believe his anger still fulminates behind
the plaster, prowling like a ghost-father
in search of prey, ravening and blind.

Terminal House

The winter he passed, the house lay in a coma,
only the occasional chuff of the boiler
cycling on and off, like a somnolent heartbeat,

the plaintive whimpers of ancient wood and plumbing,
suggesting a submerged life within its timbers.
It was like watching him die all over again—

the house this time the patient, like a fifth member
of our family, tethered to the catheters
of electric, water. We visited the place

the way one slogs to the ICU, with small gifts
of food and magazines, sifting through its spaces
with a hospital hush as though we shouldn't wake

it from its slumber. Sometimes the house would revive
briefly, and we would invite it to our small joys:
barbecuing out on the deck despite the snow;

listening to Mozart, Beiderbecke; telling tales
of when its owner was alive, bent over oak
with his beloved Japanese saw or going on

endlessly about the lost world of his youth. Spring's
fitful tauntings saw us unpacking lily bulbs
and seeds. We weeded angrily, yanking out tufts

of wild onion and crabgrass as though furious
with its encroachment on our funereal turf,
as though each stray growth were a tumor we excised

with the heart's unforgiving trephine. The house stayed
aloof from our toil, falling into disrepair,
mourning its loss despite all our ministrations,

half awake, burbling to us sometimes at night,
sobbing towards its demise, as though it understood
no one's ever anything better than human.

Manatee

Not everything's deep. Like this manatee,
propeller-scarred, slumped in the marina,
head abutting the red speedboat's rotor
as though beseeching it for more abuse.

It loves lolling on the surface, munching
lettuce thrown by tourists or lazily
chomping mangrove leaves and turtle grass.
Watching it sprawl and sway aimlessly

I feel the manatee within me rise,
that part of me that's taken body blows
as I mooched in the sea lanes of my life
where I could slouch forever easily,

immobile, adrift, never diving deep,
even though I can submarine for hours.
Oh, but the surface is sunny, placid,
filled with the faces of happy humans

amused, not by my antics, but by my
docility. Truly, I do nothing,
am evolution's greatest joke, bloated
hunkering boulder of pure fat, a beast

who lives to feast and loaf in lassitude.
Having no ambitions is a prayer
as well, sad and glorious refusal
to accept profundity as my lot.

Like the manatee, I'm identified
by my scars: Their rubric is the gashes
on their backs, inflicted by speedboats;
but *I* am recognized by the marks

on my head, the superficial wounds
of cruelty or indifference
from those I might have loved who have moved on
in their racing boats to more glorious lives

of aspiration, renown. Shallowness
is also a place where you can reside,
shiftless in the tide. Next time you joyride
and you crash into what you think's a log,

remember some of us float above the fray,
that for a manatee a good day's defined
precisely by what we do not do,
that the shoals, the shoals are teeming with life.

Night Cleaning

My mother in the night has work to do,
sequestered in Queens with disinfectant,
dust buster and vacuum cleaner. Her world
in disarray, she labors in the dark
to put things right, which is so sadly wrong

it makes me want to hold her frail body,
pressing those thin arms to her side, keep her
from snatching all the paraphernalia
of order and renewal. It's entropy
that drags her from her rest, fever dreams

of whiteness that roil her sleep, command her
to mop the kitchen floor at 3 a.m.,
squeegee the spotless windows, which stare back
with her own face in startled disbelief.
If cleanliness is next to godliness,

she will rise up, vaporous, to heaven
and immediately begin brooming clouds,
buffing the Pearly Gates. It was no joke,
though, when, at six years old, I lay in bed
hearing her vacuuming the living room,

dimly understood the enormity
of all she was trying to rectify—
the obscene childhood, the failed marriage,
—and knew her tidiness was erasure
of every stain and spot that thwarted her

hoped-for ascension to a happiness
that was always modest in its goals.
I think of her now cleaning endlessly
the small apartment where she lives, rubbing
fiercely with a sponge the already

immaculate surfaces of a world
so irreproachable it is as though
she would abrade away her existence
and leave behind nothing but cleanliness,
a shapely void where a life should have been.

Owe

Not the *Oh!* of astonishment,
but the *owe* of dereliction
of frail earthly duty we can't
fulfill, like paying back a loan

or reimbursing an emotion
offered unconditionally,
as between new lovers. We shun
indebtedness in all its gray

deshabille, its tawdry claim on
our time and the way it has
of diminishing us, undone
by our shortage of caring, cash

or a thousand other lacks. We
are everything we owe, and what
we owe is insurmountably
awesome, an elephant of debt

crashing through our lives on the veldt
of self-recrimination. We
would kill it in its tracks if we could,
take those tusks of pristine ivory

and turn them into coin, and pay
out lavishly all that we need
to give. On every human day
we count our nickels and put paid,

if we can, to the onerous weight
of responsibility. When
at last our ship comes in, its freight
is never according to plan,

never the superabundance
for which we'd hoped, but rather dross
that leads us to the acceptance
of our unflagging want for redress

from debts we bear. To owe is human,
lovely; our worries are divine
retribution. All of it won
through excess, loss and one thin dime.

Shelling

Full moon inhales the tide tonight, leaving the shore
breathless with papery lightning whelk egg cases—
ropy, corkscrewed intestines crackling underfoot

where the gray flats deliquesce to the horizon,
desert-anonymous, though brimming furtively
with beached life. I wake my logy son in time

for shelling, when the truly avaricious
rise in search of junonia, alphabet cones,
and fragile paper figs. Over calcium wreckage,

with rakes and buckets, we tentatively amass
the moonlit dead, a mummified palette
of abandoned mollusk homes, each a work of art

with no discernible artisan. By law one can only reclaim
abandoned domiciles: paired blanched angel wings
bereft of seraphim, the antlered horse conch

shed of its equine core. My son proudly displays
a banded tulip which he hoists above the surf
until, from its whorled den, a slow unfurling

of gelatinous suckered arms slowly reveals
a baby octopus that's cadged a makeshift home.
He pokes it with a stick, a boy's questioning.

The cephalopod spurts jet ink and scoots away,
leaving behind a writhing limb. My son pursues it,
trying vainly to coax it back into its abode.

I killed it, he moans and flops down on the sand.
Later we arrange our plunder on the deck,
calico scallops in a hued panoply

that dazzles the eye with its fecundity.
My son's lost in thought, curled in his own brittle shell
of self-recrimination. He has killed today

and slain, as well, something in himself that cannot
be reclaimed. Tendriled clouds sweep over the moon's
baleful eye as he slumps on the edge of the bed

and turns from the shells to look up at the sky
asking—inconsolably—*Why, Dad,*
why is it that clouds have tentacles?

Shopping Without a List

Because our hunger is endless, our needs
are endless, too, and because food
only provides temporary solace
for that relentless appetite for all
within us that cannot be simply fed,
it never quite answers to our desires
for sustenance but merely buoys us up
until the finish line of the next meal.
Perhaps that's why our shopping lists
are always provisional, missing,
invariably, some primal staple,
so we find ourselves overstocked

with fare that isn't really food—chutney,
habanero sauce, mayonnaise, relish—
while bread, butter, milk and eggs go lacking.
So I've taken to shopping in the dark,
without a list, at night, after dinner,
when hunger is no longer at my shoulder
nudging me to Oreos and Hershey bars.
Zen shopping, if you will: desireless,
more perusal than acquisition,
the supermarket as exhibition,
like America itself, brimming with
harvest and bare of satisfactions.

I troll my gaping cart along the aisles
in search of nothing—satisfied, amazed
at the profusion of comestibles,
the endless provender castling upward
to heaven on its ziggurat of shelves.
Without a list I am liberated
to buy the basics—pasta, oats and cheese—
and peruse the rest as a museum

of desires. Glorious jars of olives,
artichoke hearts and fire-roasted peppers
glow like gems in display cases. The vast
profusion of meats at the deli counter

is a fascinating, vertiginous
exhibit of how many different ways
one can spell *salami*. I pass it by,
to pick up dodgy standards like corn meal,
oil and lettuce. It's invigorating,
this paucity. The paradox of choice is that
we end up impoverished in perplexity.
But not tonight, as I free-range among
the aisles in search of nothing but my bliss.
Arriving home, the kids go through the bags
appalled at the lack of snacks, the absence
of anything they might consider food.

You call this shopping? My son says to me,
and my wife concurs. It's hard to explain
the sweet, negative capability
that guided me as I unpack the few
items I brought home: a roll call of need,
not want—flour, ground beef, oranges,
the pantry's lackluster nuts and bolts.
There's nothing to snack on! Desire's like that,
a gnawing for the unavailable
pure objects of yearning, a hollow pit
in the stomach for whatever's not there,
an emptiness that's sublimely filling.

Wordless

I like the way that music isn't words,
how something terribly important survives
beyond the verbal hubbub that drowns us
daily in its pungent stew of nouns and verbs;

for, yes, listening to Bach or Coltrane—
and I mean *really listening* (the way
you do when you practically squint your ears,
as though to make them catch invisible

nuances of the sonic palette)—you find
yourself *trying* to discern semantics
buried within the aural brouhaha
of strings and brass and woodwinds, fashioning

sentences and sense from mere noise that thwarts
all single meanings as it utters itself
into the wind of this fretful, wordy world.
Last night I listened to Keith Jarrett hum

through a 40-minute piano improv,
realizing only halfway through he was
giving a lecture on the futility
of sound to speak to anything directly

but the heart. There's bliss in the not knowing,
his accumulated notes seemed to say,
a kind of release from the nominal
and monumental weight of any defined

moment in time. It's *the nothing that is,*
as Stevens once wrote, enamored as he was
of a mystic wordlessness inside of words,
how it can unfurl with stories that hit you,

as they're fond of saying, "right where you live,"
because, after all, despite the language
in which we're mired, we *can* swim beyond
the embrace of words, caught in a soft net

of shadings that offers up precisely
nothing to which we can cling fast and claim
now this makes sense, and this, and this, and this.
It's all just noise, and in that realization

is something so exquisitely lovely
you can sometimes feel your body shaken
to its bones by a vast futility,
that refusal of all things to kowtow

to an absolute, immanent meaning
that closes doors on the unknown. I like
how the musics of this world are wordless,
how they sing to us, in constant surmise,

continuing fugues of each blessed thing
we can never say or know for certain,
how, while we love our language, we are made
of so much more that words cannot contain

and can celebrate that uncertainty
sometimes in music, which communicates
hopelessly from the world's furthest margins
an ongoing fanfare of the possible.

Acknowledgments

Alaska Quarterly Review: "Teabags"
American Arts Quarterly: "Ad"
Atlanta Review: "Vanishing House"
Bellevue Literary Review: "Terminal House"
Clackamas Literary Review: "Debt," "Playground"
Edison Literary Review: "Under Covers"
Evansville Review: "Spaghetti and Ketchup"
Fifth Wednesday Journal: "Skin," "Sorry"
Measure: "A Capella," "Surfeit"
Minetta Review: "The Weather Pig"
Mudfish: "Shelling," "Aftermath"
Notre Dame Review: "Earthward"
Poet Lore: "Shopping Without a List"
Poetry East: "Little Entropic Prayer"
Prairie Schooner: "The Fool"
Raintown Review: "Shrapnel"
River Styx: "Delivery," "The Cancer Chef"
Southwest Review: "Gorilla"
Tar River Poetry: "Cigarette," "If Only," "Wordless," "The Wrong Note"

Cover artwork, "to the light," by petr0; cover and interior book design by Diane Kistner; Adobe Garamond Pro text and titling

About FutureCycle Press

FutureCycle Press is dedicated to publishing lasting English-language poetry books, chapbooks, and anthologies in both print-on-demand and Kindle editions. Founded in 2007 by long-time independent editor/publishers and partners Diane Kistner and Robert S. King, the press incorporated as a nonprofit in 2012. A number of our editors are distinguished poets and writers in their own right, and we have been actively involved in the small press movement going back to the early seventies.

The FutureCycle Poetry Book Prize and honorarium is awarded annually for the best full-length volume of poetry we publish in a calendar year. Introduced in 2013, our Good Works projects are anthologies devoted to issues of universal significance, with all proceeds donated to a related worthy cause. Our Selected Poems series highlights contemporary poets with a substantial body of work to their credit; with this series we strive to resurrect work that has had limited distribution and is now out of print.

We are dedicated to giving all of the authors we publish the care their work deserves, making our catalog of titles the most diverse and distinguished it can be, and paying forward any earnings to fund more great books.

We've learned a few things about independent publishing over the years. We've also evolved a unique, resilient publishing model that allows us to focus mainly on vetting and preserving for posterity the most books of exceptional quality without becoming overwhelmed with bookkeeping and mailing, fundraising activities, or taxing editorial and production "bubbles." To find out more about what we are doing, come see us at www.futurecycle.org.

The FutureCycle Poetry Book Prize

All full-length volumes of poetry published by FutureCycle Press in a given calendar year are considered for the annual FutureCycle Poetry Book Prize. This allows us to consider each submission on its own merits, outside of the context of a contest. Too, the judges see the finished book, which will have benefitted from the beautiful book design and strong editorial gloss we are famous for.

The book ranked the best in judging is announced as the prize-winner in the subsequent year. There is no fixed monetary award; instead, the winning poet receives an honorarium of 20% of the total net royalties from all poetry books and chapbooks the press sold online in the year the winning book was published. The winner is also accorded the honor of being on the panel of judges for the next year's competition; all judges receive copies of all contending books to keep for their personal library.

Made in the USA
Charleston, SC
16 January 2015